KB272900

An exploratory study about the relationship between teacher's beliefs about Communicative Language Teaching (CLT) and their instructional practices

의사소통을 위한 언어 교육에 대한
원어민 교사의 생각과
실제 행동 관계 연구

의사소통을 위한 언어 교육에 대한 원어민 교사의 생각과 실제 행동 관계 연구

An exploratory study about the relationship between teacher's beliefs about Communicative Language Teaching(CLT) and their instructional practices

HyonSuk Cho

서 문

수많은 영어 학원과 늘어나는 원어민 교사의 수는 한국의 영어 배우기 열풍을 대변하는 단면이다. 어린이부터 어른까지 영어로 의사소통하기 위해 새벽부터 밤까지 영어 학원은 붐빈다. 하지만 많은 원어민 교사들이 의사소통을 위한 언어 교수법 (Communicative Language Teaching: CLT)의 개념과 동떨어진 방식으로 수업을 진행한다.

많은 영어 학습관련 연구는 교사가 무엇을 생각하는지 왜 그런지에 대한 점을 간과 하였다. 교사의 내재된 생각이나 태도가 그들의 실제 행동을 이해하는데 큰 도움이 되는 중요한 부분이므로 연구가 필요하다.

이 연구의 목적은 영어권 출신의 외국인 교사가 CLT에 대해 갖고 있는 생각과 실제 행동 간의 관계를 연구하기 위한 것이다. 이 실험적인 연구가 EFL 환경에서 학원 교사의 신념과 행동의 관계에 대한 향후 논문의 시작점이 되길 바라고, 교사의 실제 행동과 결과보다는 내재해 있고 스스로 추구하는 신념에 대한 깊은 관심과 연구가 이루어지길 바란다.

영어로 쓴 논문을 출판해 주신 한국학술정보㈜ 채종준 사장님과 편집과 출판 전 과정에 도움을 주신 강진이 선생님께 감사드린다.

Acknowledgements

This work would not have been possible without the support and assistance from a lot of people. To begin with, I would like to express my deep and sincere gratitude to my advisor, Professor Michele Milner. Her wide knowledge and her logical way of thinking have been of great value for me. Her understanding, encouraging and personal guidance have provided a good basis for the present thesis. I feel privileged to have been able to work with her.

I am grateful to the consistent valuable support from the professor Christian, Kim who always guides me along the right pathway in my research, and I am also thankful to the professors in the TESOL Graduate School at Dankook University: Dean. Jeong Sang Lee, Director of TESOL Graduate School, Prof. Young Park. Furthermore, I would also like to thank all the members of TESOL administration: Mr. Park and Mr. Lee for their supports and comments.

By far the greatest debt of gratitude is due to teachers and managers of YBM Yeoksam who allowed the observations and participated in the surveys.

I would like to address my very special thanks to my friends Kiwon Nam, KiYoung Yun, EunYoung Kim, Yunna Cho, SungWook Kim and Yumi Park who gave me helpful advices and comments, and my coworkers especially ChanKyung Park who supported me to work and study at the same time.

Finally, my special appreciation goes to my parents ChungHo Cho, MyungJin Chung, my sister InSuk Cho, and my brother WonSeo Cho for their life-long love and support. I express my very special thanks to my parents for offering their encouragement and assistance. Without them, this work could not have been completed.

Hyon-suk Cho

February, 2007

Table of contents

Ⅰ. INTRODUCTION

The need for good communication skills in English has increased around the world, and many Korean learners also want to be fluent in English for better school and work performance, for job placements or for higher score on University entrance exams.

Until the 1990s, most of the middle and high schools in Korea, where adult learners learnt English, used traditional English teaching methods such as grammar-translation, the audio-lingual method or repetition drills. In most of the classrooms, teachers taught grammar rules using direct instruction, and students practiced by memorizing grammatically correct sentences. Teachers pronounced words and learners repeated them. Also teachers would have learners read a passage and translate it. All of these cases are examples of non-communicative language teaching. Grammatical competence and accurate pronunciation were regarded as the most important parts of English proficiency, and it was commonly believed that this competence could be achieved through repetitive practice and drilling. At that time, English learning focused on tests, not actual communication.

Students who have learnt English in these traditional ways, now go to private English institutes to learn how to really communicate in various situations. Private institutions are different from public education in many ways such as; teaching style; class size; school rules; teaching goals; and the organization of learners in terms of proficiency level, age, and background. Learning materials, such as course books or other outside materials are also different: they are more communicative and often include authentic texts as compared to the textbooks used at middle and high schools.

Despite the presence of many factors more conducive to communicative teaching and learning at English institutes, not all classes meet the goals of Communicative Language Teaching(CLT). At one branch of the biggest private English institutes for adult learners in Korea, located in the center of the business area in Seoul, I, as a student, found that some teachers taught communicatively, but some did not. Native-speaker(NS) teachers at the English institute are required to teach English communicatively as indicated by short guidelines published by the institute. The guidelines describe the degree of textbook use, the amount of grammar teaching for each class, types of communicative activities and also strictly prohibit the use of Korean.

These guidelines can be seen as an external factor that influences actual classroom practice. The teacher's backgrounds are also an important variable when looking at teachers' behavior in the classroom. Although there are many cases of inexperienced and untrained teacher working in Korea, the teacher in this institute all must have a degree, teaching training, or teaching experience. It is considered that the NS teachers are familiar with CLT and have their own interpretation of CLT from their teaching experience.

Despite the guidelines of the institute and similar teaching backgrounds that emphasized CLT, some teachers at the institute, teach non-communicatively. Why did some teachers teach in a way that was different from the stated goals of communicative language teaching? I wondered if teacher's beliefs about Communicative Language Teaching(CLT) were related.

Even though CLT is increasingly popular due to an emphasis on communication in terms of proficiency, there have not been many studies on teacher's beliefs about CLT. During the last two decades research on teaching has gradually focused on teacher's beliefs and attitude that underlie teacher's classroom practice as a way to understand their behaviors in the classroom(Calderhead, 1996, Carter, 1990).

As Kleinsasser and Savignon(1991: 299) argue, "In our quest for the improvement of language teaching, we have overlooked the language teacher. Exploration······of teachers' perceptions of what they do and why they do it, holds promise for understanding the frequently noted discrepancies between theoretical understanding of second / foreign language acquisition and classroom practice" (cited in Kravas-Doukas, 1996: 188). It seemed clear that the study about teachers' underlying beliefs was needed to understand their classroom practices, and to examine the gap between teachers' theoretical beliefs about CLT and their classroom practices.

Kravas-Doukas(1996) developed a teachers' attitude scale to examine attitudes towards the communicative approach of EFL teachers in Greek public secondary schools. Her reason for this study comes from research on curriculum innovation and implementation that suggested the cause of the difference between prescribed theory and actual classroom practice was teachers' attitudes towards the communicative approach.

The study reported here is based on the assumption that teachers' actual behaviors are consistent with their beliefs, so teachers' beliefs have positive relationship with their actual practice. Generally, teachers' behaviors are determined by their beliefs since beliefs are representations of teacher's knowledge, thoughts, judgments, and decisions. There are some researchers who study to identify the relationship between beliefs and practice. Richards(2000) refers that teachers' beliefs are the fundamental source of teachers' classroom practices. Also Shavelson and Stern(1981) claim that what teachers do is managed by what they think, and teachers' theories and beliefs serve as a filter for instructional judgments and decisions(Cited in Richards, 2000).

The other assumption of this study is that in case teachers' classroom practices are inconsistent with their beliefs it is because of external factors such as school policy, learners' level or teachers' background. Pennington, et al.(1996) analyzed the gap between teachers' beliefs and actual practices caused by factors from students, teachers, and outside.

This study looks at the relationship between teacher's beliefs and practice in the Korean context to see if teachers' practices differ from their beliefs about CLT. If differences are found the factors causing the difference will also be investigated. CLT has many facets but this study will focus on grammar instructions, materials usage and activities since these are also mentioned in the institute guideline.

The aim of this study is to examine native-speaker teachers' beliefs and the relationship between teacher's beliefs and their classroom practice. It is hoped this exploratory study will point a direction for future research in this area in an EFL setting. This study will explore what beliefs EFL teachers in Korea have about what instructional practices and materials will be used and how they are applied to actual classroom in a communicative language learning setting. Thus research questions for the study are as follows:

1. What beliefs about Communicative Language Teaching(CLT) do native-speaker teachers in Korea have?
2. How are the teachers' beliefs about CLT reflected in their instructional practices in the classroom?
3. If incompatibilities exist between teacher's beliefs and practices, what factors would cause them?

II. REVIEW OF THE LITERATURE

1. Teacher's beliefs and the relationship between teacher's beliefs and practices

The study of teacher's beliefs help to understand the process of teacher's practice, so in order to investigate significant and profound insight into the teacher's practice, teacher's beliefs should be studied. Since beliefs are implicit, conceptual, and personal, they are difficult to define. However, attempts to define them by Borg(2001) who says that a belief is that the individual accepts as true consciously or unconsciously, and that it serves as a guide to thought and behavior.

In connection with beliefs in general, Borg(2001) explains that teacher's beliefs' refer to teachers' pedagogic beliefs, or beliefs related to an individual's teaching. According to Clark and Peterson(1986), the teacher sees the beliefs as conceptually acceptable reality, which guides teacher's thoughts and actions, planning and decision-making(cited in Borg, 2001). Johnson(1992) also defines teacher's beliefs as representations of the teacher's personal and professional knowledge that indirectly guides them when experiencing and responding to reality. Richards(2000) also notes that teachers' beliefs are values that teachers have in relation to content, to the process of teaching, and as a way of understanding their roles. These beliefs in turn, serve as the 'background of their decision making and action.'

Recently the importance of cognitive aspects which include language teachers' beliefs, thoughts, judgments, and decisions about teaching has also been recognized.(Richards & Lockhart 1996: Clark and Peterson 1986) Richards and Lockhart(1996) claim, "What teachers do is a reflection of what they know and believe." Despite the importance of teachers' beliefs, they have not been given much attention in past studies. Pajares(1992) emphasizes that attention to teacher's beliefs can inform educational practice and is essential to improving their professional preparation and teaching practice.

During the past 25 years teacher education research has made considerable advances in studying teacher beliefs, and analyzing connections between teacher's beliefs and practices.(see e.g., Calderhead, 1996; Thompson, 1992; Richards, Tung, & Ng, 1992; Richards & Mahoney, 1996; Johnson, 1992). Johnson(1994) argues that only since the late 80s and early 90s, researchers have started to move from only studying teaching behaviors to the consideration of the influence of teachers' thoughts, decision and judgments on language instruction.

In exploring the relationships between teachers' beliefs and classroom practice, some researchers have found a positive influence of teacher's beliefs to their practice. This means that their practices in the classroom are consistent with their expressed beliefs. Cummins(1998) conducted a case study with four teachers and reported that there was a significant relationship between teachers' beliefs and teacher activities(i.e., the beliefs the teachers held influenced their behaviors in the classroom) (cited Cummins, et al, 2004). Smith(1996), in another Canadian study of ESL teachers in postsecondary ESL classes, found that teachers' instructional decisions were correspondent with expressed beliefs, and that personal belief systems affected their way of teaching while trying to meet their institution's objectives that they were assigned to teach(Cited in Richards, 2000). Burns(1992) also identifies a center of underlying beliefs influence teachers' language teaching approach and instructional practices by investigating six ESL teachers(Cited in Richards, 2000). Moreover, Johnson (1992) observed teachers while teaching, and he found the majority of their lessons were consistent with their beliefs(Cited in Richards, 2000).

On the contrary, some researchers have shown that there is not a high degree of consistency between teacher's beliefs and their classroom practices. In the study of Pennington, et al(1996), differences were found between teachers' ideal views about teaching writing and their actual classroom practices (self-reported). A survey was conducted for teachers from five countries in the Asia-Pacific region, and while actual practices of teachers in New Zealand and Australia were close to their ideal views about teaching writing, among teachers from Hong Kong, Singapore, and Japan, a gap existed between teachers' perceived ideal classroom practices and their self-reported actual classroom behaviors. Pennington, et al.(1996) analyzed this gap as being caused by factors from students, teachers, and the outside such as a) students' level of English, motivation, and their expectations about teaching or learning; b) teachers' knowledge and perceptions about writing practice; c) environmental constraints of class size, workload, time, and external requirements such as examinations or other syllabus requirements(cited in Lockhart, 1996).

Inconsistencies between teachers' beliefs and their classroom practices were also shown by Duffy(1982)'s research. Factors that restrain teachers from maintaining their beliefs are a) social forces within the classroom; b) external constraints such as prescribed textbooks and materials, pressures to "teach to the test," and expectations from parents and the community; and c) pressure on teachers because they have too much to do or manage in the classroom(cited in Lockhart, 1996).

1) Empirical studies on the relationship between teacher's beliefs about CLT and practices

A number of studies have looked specifically at the relationship between teachers' beliefs and their classroom practice with respect to CLT. Karavas-Doukas(1996) conducted an attitude survey on fourteen Greek teachers of English to find teachers' beliefs about Communicative Language Teaching. Her study examined beliefs and attitudes about 5 aspects of CLT: group / pair work, quality and quantity of error correction, the role and contribution of learners in the learning process, the role of the teacher in the classroom, and place / importance of grammar using an attitude scale and classroom observations. The study revealed differences between the practices and beliefs, specifically that teachers displayed both traditional and communicative approach in their classroom practices, with most of the lessons being teacher-fronted and focused on form rather than meaning.

Li(1998) also studied the relationship between teacher's beliefs and practices by surveying eighteen Korean secondary EFL teachers in 1995 and doing following-up interviews with ten teachers. This study attributed discrepancies between beliefs and practices to difficulties of applying CLT. The difficulties included teachers' perceived deficiencies in English, in strategic and socio-cultural knowledge, and in CLT training. Teachers also had misconceptions about CLT, and little time to develop materials for communicative classes. Difficulties were also caused by students' English proficiency and the fact that their motivation for improving communicative competence was low, so they were willing to participate in class activities. A further source of difficulties and pressure was caused by educational system, large classes, grammar-based tests, and little support for teaching(cited in Chou, 2003).

Choi(1999) investigated the communicative language teaching of English as a foreign language from teachers' views in Korea middle school classrooms in order to see if there was a gap between theoretical views that teachers expressed and their actual behavior. The purpose of this study was to explore Korean teachers' beliefs about the main objectives of English teaching as well as teachers' practices in CLT classroom instruction. The result showed that there were some discrepancies between teachers' beliefs about CLT and their practices. Teacher-self reported documents demonstrated that their teaching practices in classroom instructions were still largely teacher-centered, and drill-driven rather than learner-centered.(cited in Chou, 2003).

2. Communicative Language Teaching in the classroom

In his review of teaching methodologies, Richards(2004) looked at traditional approaches and communicative language teaching. This overview showed that up to the late 1960s, traditional approaches to language teaching focused on grammatical competence, and it was believed that grammar could be learned through direct instruction and through repetitive practice and drilling. During 1970s to 1990s, fluency was more emphasized than accuracy, but since 1990s, teachers have been recommended to balance fluency and accuracy.

Communicative language teaching has been interpreted in many ways, in terms of teaching conversation, an absence of grammar in the class, or a focus on free-discussion as a main activity. CLT includes notion of grammatical competence which includes knowledge the language itself, and encompasses both its form and meaning. Stern(1983) states that language learners should know the rules of the language and be able to use them without consciously paying attention to them(Cited in Hedge, 2000). Savignon (2002) believes that linguistic competence, or 'grammatical competence', is demonstrated 'not by stating a rule but by using a rule in the interpretation, expression, or negotiation of meaning.' This definition includes an emphasis on form and meaning and usage.

One important point of grammatical competence is, as Faerch, Haastrup, and Phillipson(1984, cited in Hedge, 2000) affirm, that a communicatively competent person should be linguistically competent, however this does not mean that a person who has a high degree of accuracy in the use of the rules automatically has achieved communicative competence.

Views about the importance of the ability to understand language teaching in terms of form and meaning have shaped how CLT has developed. Thus grammar teaching in CLT should be communicative and emphasize both form and meaning. Savignon(1991) notes that teacher should not 'forsake' of grammar. Rather the replacement of language laboratory structure drills with meaning-focused self-expression is found to be a more effective way to develop grammar competence.

To achieve grammatical competence for communication, some researchers suggest about materials usage to connect grammar books and communicative books. Cunningsworth(1998) says that many students will benefit from additional material that gives explanations and rules in straightforward language, together with practice exercises on each grammar point. A good example of this type of material is *English Grammar in Use*(Murphy 1994), but the exercises in grammar books are usually made up of isolated sentences, so they are not examples of communicative language. For this reason, Cunningsworth (1998) suggests, "Grammar books and most other supplementary materials are best used in connection with communicative coursebooks and not on their own."(p.139).

In CLT, the importance of group work has been emphasized to develop communicative skills and to empower learners. As Chou(2003) states, students are expected to interact with one another through group work. CLT favors interaction among small numbers of students in order to maximize the time each student has to learn through meaningful negotiation and discussion. Group work activity has several benefits. For example, learners can learn a language by listening to the speech of other members of the group. Thus learners can increase their motivation, and also increase the amount of time to speak for communicating as opposed to teacher-fronted activities.

There are many ways to implement group work activities in a CLT class, Brown(1994) suggests that teachers use teaching resource books as well as the textbooks. Richards(2000) suggests a variety of ways that teachers can make use of the textbook itself. They can use the textbook page by page following the teacher's manual, or a teacher might choose a topic from the book and use his or her own materials to supplement to replace the presentation in the book, or a teacher might employ other textbooks or resource books.

Communicative Language Teaching has dealt with communicative practice (where language is used in a real communicative context, where real information is exchanged and where no language is predictable) while mechanical practice (which is controlled practice that students perform without understanding the language they use) were mainly used in traditional approaches. In the decades of the 40s, 50s, and 60s, language materials contained the drill, but recent books avoid the drill[1] and increase communicative activity. Brown(1994) notes that drilling may occur in CLT, but additionally not centrally, and dialogs, if used, center around communicative functions and are not normally memorized.

Another characteristic of CLT is authenticity. Since language learning has put stress on preparation for the real world, the connection between classroom activities and real life has been regarded as an important issue for communicative language teaching. In CLT, it is considered "desirable to give learners the opportunity to respond to genuine communicative needs in realistic situations so that they develop strategies for understanding language as actually used by native speakers(Larsen-Freeman, 2000, p.132). Clarke and Silbertstein (1977: 52) comment, "Classroom activities should parallel the 'real world' as closely as possible. Since language is a tool of communication, methods and materials should concentrate on the message and not the medium. The purposes of reading should be the same in class as they are in real life."(cited in Richards, 2004: 21)

Brown(1994) notes, "By introducing natural texts rather than concocted, artificial material, students will more readily dive in to

---

[1] A drill may be defined as a technique that focuses on a minimal number of language forms. Repetition drills and substitution drills simply require that the students repeat a word or phrase whether the student understands it or not, so they are not communicative.(Brown, 1994)

the activity."(p.245). To make a class more authentic and more appropriated for the real-life, teachers could use various range of materials from newspapers, magazines or internet and develop activities or tasks according to students' level and interest (Tomlinson, 1998). Maley(1998) suggests some ideas about authentic materials usage. Authentic texts could be used for interpretation that students engage with the text on a personal level, or could be used for more extended practical activity, or could be reformulated in a different form with the same meaning.

The use of authentic materials for communicative language teaching have been said to have both strength and weakness. Advocator of authentic materials claim that authentic materials help learners' use of English in the real world, and generate a learning strategy not only for English but other subjects (Wong, Kwok and Choi, 1995)

However, others have pointed out problems when using authentic materials in the classroom. Richards(2001) points out, "Authentic materials often contain difficult language, unneeded vocabulary items and complex language structures which causes a burden for the teacher in lower-level classes."(p.253). For this reason, Guariento and Moley(2001) suggest that authentic materials should be used according to learners' ability. Likewise, Maria(2002) suggests that since authentic materials are 'unedited and remain un-simplified', the language in them should be used in manageable quantities and should emphasize comprehensibility. Further, he states that teachers who use authentic materials should determine their 'applicability and adaptability' for the classroom use.

Richard(2004) also proposes that teachers should use authentic materials that are appropriate for the linguistic abilities of their learners.

Despite the perceived beliefs of using authentic materials, many teachers cannot use them due to external factors such as time, money, and school policy, teachers use textbooks in the communicative classroom. "The textbook is an almost universal element of ELT teaching."(Hutchinson and Torres, 1994: 315). Textbooks are one of the easily accessible and prevailing materials, but there are many debates on using textbooks. Since textbooks can be systematic, some researchers state advantages of textbook use. Hutchinson and Torres (1994) equate that commercial materials offer a more systematic and carefully designed syllabus based on a long history of education. Harmer(1991) also mentions textbooks are systematic about the amount of vocabulary(Cited in Richards, 1993).

On the contrary, some are against using textbooks due to limited content, activities, and texts. Thanasolulas(1999) indicates that when a teacher follows a regular pattern: reading a text, asking some questions, and discussing learners would be fed up with the process. Allwright(1990) similarly states teachers cannot directly use the textbooks because the textbooks are inflexible. In this manner, Richards(2000) discourages the use of textbooks that are less relevant and appropriate than teacher-made materials.

For teachers' advantages of using a textbook are explained by Richards (2000) who claims, "The practical benefits teachers gain from using textbooks in terms of time benefits and access to a varied choice of professionally produced resources(p.129)."

Hutchinson and Torres(1994) admit the teacher benefits from using textbooks by stating, "it saves time, gives direction to lessons, guides discussion, facilitates giving of homework, making teaching easier, better organized, more convenient, and learning easier, faster, better. Most of all the textbook provides confidence and security."(p.318).

However, Freeman and Porter(cited in Studolsky 1989 as citied in Richards, 2000) studied how teachers use textbooks and found that even when the textbooks determine the sequence of topics to be taught, teachers still have to decide time allocation, expected performance, and modify instruction to fit different student abilities. Therefore, Studolsky(1989) comments that teachers' abilities to teach and to employ pedagogical reasoning skills are not nega-tively affected by the use of a textbook. The book served simply as a resource (cited in Richards 2000).

The use of textbooks has advantages and disadvantages at the same time as previously discussed. According to Garinger(2001), using only textbooks page by page without supplementing or modifying is not the most satisfactory method for meeting students' needs for learning from various sources, but on the other hand both teachers and students can build framework for teaching and learning through textbooks. In consequence, Garinger refers that it is important that teachers balance between being "a servant of textbooks" and "A master of textbooks." Teachers should control the use of textbooks, not be controlled by the textbooks.

Based on the theory of CLT which are form and meaning focused grammar teaching, encouragement of group work activities and communicative activities, and authentic materials usage, teachers have beliefs about what instructions, activities and materials are needed and developed, and decide how well they apply to the actual classrooms. Therefore, how teachers believe about CLT affect how they do in the classrooms a great deal.

Ⅲ. METHODOLOGY

1. The Current Study

Previous empirical studies about the relationship between teacher's beliefs about Communicative Language Teaching(CLT) and practices showed that teacher's beliefs were closely interrelated with teacher's behavior, but there were some discrepancies between teacher's beliefs about CLT and their practices. The aim of this exploratory study was to examine teacher's beliefs and practices in an EFL communicative language class. Few studies had been conducted on the subject of native-speaker(NS) teachers' beliefs in a foreign language setting, thus this current study investigated the relationship between NS teachers' beliefs about CLT and their practices at an institute in Korea.

The first hypothesis of this study was that teachers' actual behaviors were consistent with their beliefs, so in this sense teachers' beliefs had a positive relationship with their actual practice. The assumption behind this hypothesis was that teachers' behaviors were determined by their beliefs since beliefs were representations of teacher's knowledge, thoughts, judgments, and decisions.

The second hypothesis was that in case teachers' classroom practices were inconsistent with their beliefs it was because of external factors. Teachers' classroom practices were sometimes inconsistent with their beliefs, but reflected other outside factors such as school policy or teachers' background.

Research questions in this study were 1) What beliefs about Communicative Language Teaching do native-speaker teachers at an institute in Korea have? 2) How are the teachers' beliefs about CLT reflected in their instructional practices in the classroom? 3) If incompatibilities exist between teacher's beliefs and practices, what factors would cause them?

An attitude scale questionnaire was developed to explore the beliefs about Communicative Language Teaching NS teachers at an English institute had. The closed-questionnaire using attitude scale was first piloted to check item validity then revision was distributed to teachers at the institute. To examine the relationship between teachers' beliefs as expressed in the questionnaire, and their actual practices in the classroom, a classroom observation sheet was developed so that comparisons could be made between the two. After identifying consistent and inconsistent aspects of the relationship, a follow-up open-ended questionnaire was carried out.

2. Participants

The pilot survey was given to five native English teachers from USA, Australia, and Canada, who were not teachers of the language institute where the actual survey was distributed.

The revised closed-questionnaire using attitude scales(see appendix 1) was distributed to 20 teachers at the language institute to explore teachers' beliefs about CLT. The participants were all from English-speaking countries; USA, Australia, and Canada, and 50% were female and 50% were male. All the participants were equipped with 1 ~ 17 years teaching experience and with a degree or training related to ESL / EFL teaching methods.

Of the teachers who were surveyed, classroom observations(see appendix 3) were conducted with four of them in order to examine the consistency and inconsistency between the teachers' expressed beliefs and their actual classroom practices. Two of the observed teachers were female from Canada, and the other two were male from Ireland and America. One of four teachers had been taking an online master program of Applied Linguistics, and the others had TEFL certification. All had teaching experience for more than 3 years. All four teachers, who were observed, were asked to complete an open-ended questionnaire(see appendix 2) to further investigate the relationship between teacher's expressed beliefs and observed practices.

3. Instrument

In order to explore teachers' beliefs about CLT, a Likert-type scale(or method of summated ratings) was used in this study. According to Karavas-Doukas(1996), the Likert-type scale provided a very useful and relatively uncomplicated method of obtaining data on people's attitudes. A Likert-type scale consisted of a series of declarative statements. The subjects were asked to express whether they agreed or disagreed with each statement. Five columns were next to each items consisting of 'strongly agree', 'agree', 'uncertain, undecided, or neutral', 'disagree', and 'strongly disagree'. Each column had a specific value; 5, 4, 3, 2, 1 respectively.

Respondents were asked to circle the numbers to indicate how much they agreed or disagreed with each item. A high score meant a positive attitude toward CLT. Positive statements were scored 5 for 'strongly agree' and 1 for 'strongly disagree', and for negative statements, the score was reversed; negative statements were scored 1 for 'strongly agree' and 5 for 'strongly disagree'.

It should be mentioned that a limitation of a Likert-type scale was the difficulty of judging a neutral point on the scale. As Oppenheim(1996) pointed out, the neutral point of the questionnaire scale was not necessarily the mid-point between the extreme scores. This was because a respondent could obtain a middle score by either being uncertain about items or by holding inconsistent or strongly positive and strongly negative attitudes towards the attitude object in question(cited in Karavas-Doukas, 1996).

The statements of the questionnaire were classified by the following aspects of CLT:

1. Grammar instruction(10 statements: 5 negative, 5 positive)
2. Group work activities(8 statements: 4 negative, 4 positive)
3. Authentic text usage(6 statements: 3 negative, 3 positive)
4. Types of activities(6 statements: 3 negative, 3 positive)

The above four sections were indicated in the teaching guidelines of the institute where the survey and classroom observation were conducted. The teaching guidelines dealt with teachers' instructional practices in a Communicative Language Teaching setting. Teachers' instructional practices of CLT included how to teach grammar and communication skills by doing various communicative activities, and how to use teaching materials such as textbooks, and authentic materials. Since this study was exploratory study about the teachers of the language institute, the thematic sections of the questionnaire were classified based on the teaching guideline, consequently other aspects of CLT were not considered in this study.

In order to test validity of the items, a pilot survey was conducted. The pilot study helped to access the clarity of the statements, and the most suitable wording. To construct a belief questionnaire or belief scales, first, a series of statements that cover four aspects of Communicative Language Teaching was composed based on the literature about CLT.(Richards 2000, Kravas-Doukas 1996, Savignon 2000, Hedge 2000) Second, the statements were distinguished between those holding favorable and those holding unfavorable attitudes. A positive statement and a negative statement were in a pair, and they had the same meaning but different wording.

The split-half method was used to determine the reliability of the study's belief scales. This was not only the most commonly used method, but measured reliability by splitting the scale into two matched halves and correlating the scores of each half(Karavas-Doukas 1996).

The analysis of the returned pool survey was carried out. The statements that the respondents answered either as 'uncertainty or neutral' or indicated as agreement or disagreement inconsistently in pair statements were modified toward extreme or clarity. It was thought that uncertainty or inconsistent choices were caused by ambiguity or uncleanness of the statements.

Based on the analysis of the pilot study, a attitude scale questionnaire(see appendix 1) was distributed to 20 teachers in a language institute in Korea. The attitude scales consisted of 30 statements(15 statements were described in a positive manner and 15 were in a negative way[2]) placed in random order.

By using the Likert-type scale or method of summated rating, the highest possible score was 150 by scoring 5, the highest mark on all 30 statements, the lowest was 30 by scoring 1, the lowest mark on all 30 statements, and the middle point was 90 achieved by being uncertain, neutral about all 30 items. The participants' scores could therefore fall within a continuum from 30 to 150.

---

[2] Positive statements are statement number 2, 5, 8, 9, 10, 16, 18, 19, 22, 23, 24, 25, 26, 29, 30, and rest are negative statements.

Of the 9 teachers who completed the attitude scale(see appendix 1), 4 of them were chosen for classroom observation because of the variety in their expressed beliefs and differences in how their classes were conducted. An observation sheet(see appendix 3) aimed at documenting and analyzing the types and characteristics of the activities carried out and the materials used in the classrooms was developed. The observation sheet(see appendix 3) was used to compare teachers' practices with their beliefs about Communicative Language Teaching, and to examine closely the teachers' practice in terms of grammar teaching, activity types, and materials use.

The observation sheet(see appendix 3) was also divided into four thematic groups; grammar instruction, group work activity, authentic texts usage, and types of activities, which matched with the four groups on the two questionnaires(see appendix 1 and 2). Each section had a column of the length of time for the following use of materials; changes made to the textbook, use of other course books, and others such as authentic materials. This time record section told what percentage of the whole class time was spent for each thematic group so that it helped to prove the consistency between statement of teachers' belief scales(see appendix 1) and classroom practices.

The open-ended questionnaire(see appendix 2) consisted of four sections: grammar instruction, group work activities, authentic text usage, and the types of activities. The questionnaire aimed to explore the classroom more in detail for consistent and inconsistent relationship between beliefs and practices. In particular, the open-ended questions were more broad and general in meaning than the closed-questionnaire to elicit reason for possible discrepancies between teachers' expressed beliefs and their actual classroom practices. Since the questions were more general, teachers could be more descriptive about what they believed and what they did in their classrooms. The four teachers who were observed also completed the open-ended questionnaire(see appendix 2).

4. Data Collection

Twenty attitude scale questionnaire were distributed at the institute of which 9 were returned by email or in person, yielding a response rate of 45%. The class observation of four teachers was conducted with 4 of these 9 teachers. Each teacher was observed for two consecutive days. They were in different learners' level, one was teaching level 4, one was teaching level 7, and the others were teaching level 6.[3] The class each day was made up of a 120-minute-lesson including a 20-minute-break. The observer did not participate into the class at all as a student. The observer used the class observation sheet(see appendix 3) to record the procedures of each class.

Following the observations, the open-ended questionnaires(see appendix 2) were distributed to the observed four teachers and all were returned for a 100% response rate.

---

[3] Learner level of this institute was ranged from level 1 to level 9, and from level 1 to 3 was considered as beginning level, from 4 to 6 is as intermediate, and from 7 to 9 was as advanced level

5. Data Analysis Procedure

In order to see teachers' attitude toward CLT, the closed questionnaire(see appendix 1) using attitude scales was used. After collecting the attitude scales(see appendix 1), all the statements were divided into two parts according to positive statements and negative statements, the marked score was summed up respectively, and added a summed positive part to a summed negative one to get a total score(the score of negative statements was reversed; negative statements were scored 1 for 'strongly agree' and 5 for 'strongly disagree'). The total score implied how much the respondents had a favorable or unfavorable attitude towards CLT. The highest possible score, 150 meant the most favorable attitude towards CLT, and the lowest 30 indicated the least favorable attitude towards CLT.

The pair statements were also checked for the internal consistency of their choices. The scale of positive statement and negative statement in a pair should be consistent since they had the same meaning, but different wordings. For example, if one strongly agreed with a positive statement by marking degree 5, s / he should(strongly) disagree with a negative pair of the statement by marking 1 or 2.

To compare teachers' observed practices with their expressed beliefs, first the observation sheet(see appendix 3) was compared with the four groups of the attitude scales(see appendix 1), and the observation sheet were matched one by one with statements of the attitude scales(see appendix 1). Then consistent and inconsistent sections were grouped according to each teacher. After the comparison, discrepancies and similarities were categorized according to four aspects of CLT. The pattern of the four teachers was looked at to see if they showed any similarity in terms of what aspects of CLT produced discrepancies between beliefs and practices.

The open-ended questionnaire was used to find reasons for consistent or inconsistent behavior. For the open-ended questionnaire (see appendix 2), each teacher's responses to the open-ended questionnaire were compiled and content analyzed by comparing with the belief scales and the result of the classroom observations. Through this questionnaire, the process and the reason of the teachers' teaching practice could be explained in details. The open-ended question section provided rich and interesting information from the respondents.

Ⅳ. DISCUSSION OF RESULTS

All teachers who were native-speakers at the English institute in Korea and participated in the survey had positive attitudes towards Communicative Language Teaching. This could be seen by total scores of nine teachers ranged between 132 and 98 that were above 90 which was the middle score of the highest 150 and the lowest 30. Table 1 showed their scores of the belief scales.

Table 1: Teachers' total scores of the belief scales

Teacher	D	B	C	H	I	A	G	F	E
Total Score	132	123	118	115	115	105	103	102	98

However, some teachers marked high values on non-communicative teaching style or activities even though they, on the whole, shared high degree of positive respond towards CLT. Two teachers indicated that direct grammar explanations were necessary for communicative language teaching, and four teachers thought that non-communicative activities, for example, substitution drills, repetition drills of dialogues or questioning practice exercises, were effective for improving communicative ability. It would be further investigated through the open-ended questionnaire whether it was due to lack of understanding of theory of CLT, or other reasons.

Teacher 1's teaching was mostly consistent with her beliefs reported in the attitude scale questionnaire(see appendix 1). Teacher 1, who were in learners' level 4, taught grammar by using the textbook and other course books that she edited and changed for 15% of the class time, and gave students time to work in groups for 35% of the class time. However, she mainly used controlled practices such as substitution drills, and rarely gave learners time for free discussion. Furthermore, she did not use authentic materials at all. Table 2 showed how she spent class time.

Table 2: The observation outline for Teacher 1

Thematic group	Textbook use		Others	
	No change from the textbook	Change from the textbook	A. Other course books, B. No textbook, C. Others	
Grammar instruction	25 min(12.5%)	0 min	A. 5 min(2.5%)	
Group activities	35 min(17.5%)	0 min	A. 35 min(17.5%)	
Authentic text usage	0 min		0 min	
Types of activities	Non-communicative	Communicative	Non-communicative	Communicative
	40 min(20%)	0 min	A.10 min(5%)	B.50 min(25%)

The practice of Teacher 1 was mostly consistent with her beliefs in the belief scale(see appendix 1) Table 3 showed outline of the comparison. For the areas of 'group work activity' and 'types of activity', her actual classroom practice was same as her beliefs. She agreed with the statement that group work activities help communicative language teaching, and she spent 35% of the whole class time for group work activities. Also she used activities that she agreed in the attitude scale questionnaire(see appendix 1).

However, two things were different from her beliefs, one was terminology use. She disagreed with use of grammar rules and terminology for communicative language teaching, but she used some in the class.

Moreover, she agreed with the authentic text usage in the communicative classroom, but she used the textbook and other course books, not any authentic materials.

Generally, communicative activities were commonly used and recommended rather than non-communicative activities including repetition or drills in a communicative language teaching classroom, but surprisingly she marked high values on the statements of merits of non-communicative drills of the belief scales(see appendix 1), and she did controlled practice and substitution drills in her classroom that were non-communicative. It could be considered her confusion of the principles of CLT, but her agreement with two opposing statements was consistent, for example, the statement number 9 and 11, 27 and 30.

Table 3: Comparison of beliefs and practices for Teacher 1

Statement No. of the belief questionnaire	Category of the thematic group		Correspondence
	Teacher's Beliefs	Teacher's practice	
4, 8, 12, 17, 22, 29,	*Grammar instruction*		Different
	Rules &terminology use: Disagree	"Gerund, infinitive" terminology used	
23, 26	*Authentic text usage*		Different
	Authentic texts develop learners' language ability: Agree	No authentic text use	
2, 7, 10, 16	*Group work activities*		Same
	Group work activity helps communicative language teaching: Agree	35% of the class time	
11, 27, 9	*Types of activities*		Same*
	Repetition, substitution, controlled practice: Agree	Did controlled practices in the class	

Teacher 2's teaching was consistent with her beliefs expressed in the attitude scale questionnaire(see appendix 1) as Table 5 showed. She was teaching level 7, and spent almost same amount of time for group work activity, authentic texts use, and various activity by using teaching materials she prepared, not teaching grammar at all as Table 4 showed.

Table 4: The observation outline for Teacher 2

Thematic group	Textbook use		Others	
	No change from the textbook	Change from the textbook	A. Other coursebooks, B. No textbook, C. Others	
Grammar instruction	0 min	0 min	0 min	
Group activities	0 min	0 min	C(teacher-made). 70 min(35%)	
Authentic text usage	0 min		C(shortened newspaper article). 60 min(30%)	
Types of activities	Non-communicative	Communicative	Non-communicative	Communicative
			40 min(20%)	30 min(15%)

The activities she prepared based on the shortened newspaper articles were divided into three parts: warm-up activity, understanding of the texts, and the further group discussion. Her actual classroom behavior was same as her expressed beliefs in all areas as the Table 5 showed.

Despite the consistency between her beliefs and actual practices about CLT, it is interesting to note that she also showed consistency about activity types that would not be considered communicative. She favored with controlled practices that were non-communicative activities, and she did controlled practices while non-communicative activities such as repetition and substitution drills were not commonly encouraged to use in a CLT classroom(e.g. statement number 11, 14, and 27 of the attitude scale questionnaire).

Table 5: Comparison of beliefs and practices for Teacher 2

Statement No. of the belief questionnaire	Category of the thematic group		Correspondence
	Teacher's Beliefs	Teacher's practice	
1, 25, 20, 5, 4, 29, 17, 8, 12, 22	*Grammar instruction*		Same
	Communicative activities more than grammar teaching: Agree	No grammar teaching	
26, 23	*Authentic text usage*		Same
	Authentic texts develop learners' language ability: Agree	Mainly used: all activities were based on the authentic texts	
2, 7, 10, 13, 16, 21	*Group work activities*		Same
	Group work activity helps communicative language teaching: Agree	35% of the class time	
11, 14, 27	*Types of activities*		Same*
	Repetition, substitution, controlled practice: Agree	Did controlled practices in the class	

Teacher 3's teaching was also almost completely consistent with the beliefs he expressed in the questionnaire(see appendix 1). He mainly used the textbook(for 57.5% of the class time), and used authentic materials from the internet to supplement the textbooks, only a small amount of time. He usually started the class with grammar teaching or a listening activity from the textbook. In both cases the activity was teacher-controlled. Table 6 showed the brief result of the class observation.

Table 6: The observation outline for Teacher 3

Thematic group	Textbook use		Others
	No change from the textbook	Change from the textbook	A. Other coursebooks, B. No textbook, C. Others
Grammar instruction	15 min(7.5%)	0 min	0 min
Group activities	55 min(27.5%)	0 min	0 min
Authentic text usage	0 min		C(letters from the internet) 25 min(12.5%)
Types of activities	Non-communicative	Communicative	Non-communicative	Communicative
	35 min(17.5%)	20 min(10%)	0 min	B.50min(25%)

The comparison of teacher's behavior and teacher's beliefs indicated as Table 7 showed that his teaching had a positive relationship with his beliefs. Beliefs about grammar instructions being done before communicative activities, group work activity being changed by a teacher, and communicative activity needed instead of repetition, or controlled practice exercises were what he believed and also what he did in the class.

Table 7: The observation outline for Teacher 3

Statement No. of the belief questionnaire	Category of the thematic group		Correspondence
	Teacher's Beliefs	Teacher's practice	
29	*Grammar instruction*		Different
	Separate grammar teaching: Disagree	Did a grammar practice which included communication	
3, 6, 26, 28, 23,	*Authentic text usage*		Different
	Authentic texts develop learners' language ability: Agree	Rarely used: 12.5% of class time	

Statement No. of the belief questionnaire	Category of the thematic group		Correspondence
	Teacher's Beliefs	Teacher's practice	
1, 17, 8, 25	*Grammar instruction*		Same*
	Grammar instructions prior to communicative activities: Agree	Grammar teaching before the communicative activity	
2, 7, 10, 16, 18	*Group work activities*		Same
	Group work activities in the textbook can be changed: Agree	Skipped inefficient part	
27, 30	*Types of activities*		Same
	Non-communicative drills: Disagree	Picked up the communicative activity from the textbook	

Teacher 4's teaching was consistent with the teacher's beliefs in the expressed questionnaire(see appendix 1). Teacher 4 used only other outside materials and did not use the textbook at all. During most of the class time, group activity and discussion were done using newspaper articles. Table 8 showed the summary of his classes.

Table 8: The observation outline for Teacher 4

Thematic group	Textbook use		Others	
	No change from the textbook	Change from the textbook	A. Other course books, B. No textbook, C. Others	
Grammar instruction	0 min	0 min	0 min	
Group activities	0 min	0 min	C(newspaper) 60 min(30%)	
Authentic text usage	0 min		C(newspaper) 55 min(22.5%)	
Types of activities	Non-communicative	Communicative	Non-communicative	Communicative
	0 min	0 min	0 min	C.85min(42.5%)

He used group discussion to boost communication amongst learners with using authentic texts instead of the textbook texts, and he did not teach grammar and repetitive drills. Table 9 showed the correspondence between teacher's beliefs and his practice in the classroom during the observation.

As indicated in his attitude scale questionnaire(see appendix 1), he focused communication rather than grammar and non-communicative practices or drills. Students freely group-discussed or whole-class-discussed based on reading of the newspaper articles as agreed with the statement 19, 23, and 26 for authentic text usage, 2, 10 and 16 for group work activities, and 9 and 24 for communicative activities.

Table 9: Comparison of beliefs and practices for Teacher 4

Statement No. of the belief questionnaire	Category of the thematic group		Correspondence
	Teacher's Beliefs	Teacher's practice	
5, 8, 17, 20,	*Grammar instruction*		Same
	For high level students, no grammar teaching: Agree	No grammar teaching	
3, 6, 19, 26, 28, 23,	*Authentic text usage*		Same
	Authentic texts use: Agree	Mainly used, all activities were based on the authentic texts	
2, 7, 10, 16	*Group work activities*		Same
	Group work activities promote communication: Agree	30% of the class time	
9, 24, 27, 30	*Types of activities*		Same
	Non-communicative activities(Repetition, Q&A practice): Disagree	Communicative activities: free discussion	

Teacher 4's behavior was same as his beliefs. Since he thought the textbook was incompatible with the students overall interests and levels, and the students had high degree of knowledge of grammar, he did not use the textbook and teach grammar. He believed that group work activity, authentic materials, and communicative activity promote communicative language learning, and his class was mainly focused on them.

From the open-ended questionnaire, the reason of the differences between teachers' beliefs and actual practices were found. Teacher 1 disagreed with use of grammar rules and terminology for communicative language teaching, but she used some in the class.

The reason was by commenting found in her open-ended questionnaire that she taught grammar only when learners made same errors of grammar. It was guessed that she used the terminology such as 'gerund and infinitive' because some students made same mistakes for several times, so she decided to explain the grammar in detail with using grammar rules and terminology that could help to understand for the adult learners who had already known those terms.

Even if teacher 1 believed that authentic materials were useful because they were current and relevant, she explained in the open-ended questionnaire that lower level students needed textbooks rather than newspaper articles because more structured texts and activities could be useful for them. For this reason, she agreed with the institute set rule for the amount of textbook use for the lower levels ranging from level 1 to 6 as 40% of the class time.

The reason that she agreed with non-communicative drills and used in her classrooms were she thought that the lower level students could improve grammar skills and communicative language skills through controlled practices and repetitive drills.

Teacher 2's practices were almost consistent with her expressed beliefs. She strongly agreed with the statements 23, and 26 of the attitude scale questionnaire(see appendix 1) which stated positive influences of authentic text usage for communicative language teaching. She used shortened newspaper articles as reading texts, she explained in her open-ended questionnaire(see appendix 2) that newspaper articles help generate discussion, but the length was usually long, so she shortened the articles to have more time for discussion.

Teacher 2 who did not teach grammar, thought that grammar teaching should be done only when the communication was impossible due to insufficient or inappropriate knowledge of grammar as agreed with the statement 8, 17, and 22 of the attitude scale(see appendix 1). She commented, "I think a grammar point should be addressed in situations where the grammar error results in a communication breakdown or miscommunication. I would classify this type of situation as a 'teachable moment'."

For group work activity, she pointed out that it was effective in promoting class communication because students had more speaking time and the stronger students could help the weaker students.

For the consistency about activity types which were not considered communicative, teacher 2 explained about that by saying that lower level and beginning level students would benefit from structured activities or drills. Yet she thought that activities that simulate 'real-life' situations and tasks that force students to communicate to solve a problem together best promote communicative skills. However, due to student levels her actual classroom behavior differed from the beliefs.

Teacher 3 explained that grammar teaching prior to communicative activity should be introduced at the beginning of the class for specific grammar points and that students should be encouraged to use it in conversational activities during class.

Also he stated about textbook use, that the textbook was a useful tool in any class, but usually had to be adapted to a greater or lesser extent to suit the situation. Parts of the textbook might be omitted and supplemented. Even if the levels were the same, different classes could have different requirements and interests, so it was necessary to change the book accordingly.

For authentic materials, he was aware of their advantages that they provided authentic language experience and an alternative to the textbook, and motivating to learners. However, he claimed that they were not specifically prepared to be used for teaching situation and that they might need to be altered or adapted in someway which could be time-consuming.

In comparing the inconsistent and consistent areas between expressed beliefs and practices, some pattern emerged. All four observed teachers' practices were consistent with their expressed beliefs for the group work activities and grammar instruction. Regarding the statement number 2, 7, 10, 16 of the attitude scales(see appendix 1), they believed that the group work activities would promote communication in the classroom, and they spent more or less 30% of the class time for group work activities. Concerning the statement number 8, 17 of the attitude scales(see appendix 1), all the four teachers agreed that mastering grammar did not relate with achieving communicative competence, and they spent more or less 10% of class time for grammar instruction, two of them did not teach grammar at all.

However, two pairs, Teacher 1 and 3, Teacher 1 and 2 of the four teachers showed inconsistency between their expressed beliefs and the observed practices for authentic text usage and types of activities. T1 and T3 supported authentic text usage by agreeing with the statement 23, and 26 of the attitude scales(see appendix

1), and by writing merits of the authentic materials in the open-ended questionnaire(see appendix 3), but they used authentic texts 0% and 12.5% of the class time respectively. It could be due to the school guidelines about the amount of textbook use, teachers' time to adapt, and the characteristics of the authentic text that included words for written English or complicated sentence structures.

T1 and T2 agreed with non-communicative activities such as controlled practices or substitution drills, which were not commonly encouraged to use for CLT class, by agreeing with the statement 11 and 27, and they conducted drills which was non-communicative. It could be caused by teachers' learning experience or learners' level. Teachers tended to teach as they learnt as a student, and they used more structure activities when learners' level was low.

After considering all the comments teachers made in the open-ended questionnaire(see appendix 2), the inconsistencies between teachers' beliefs and practices were caused by factors from learners, teachers, and external constraints. Some situations of these factors restrained teachers teaching as they believed or wanted.

First, according to learners' level, teachers decided how to teach including what activity and what materials to use. When the learners' overall level was low, teachers used activities that forced students to practice a particular grammatical form because they believed lower level students could benefit from the drills and practices of forms to build up their basic skills to communicate fluently later even if CLT encouraged activities engaging learners' authentic communication.

Second, due to teachers' time and money, the gap existed between teachers' beliefs and practices. Teachers wanted to use authentic texts, but they needed to alter or adapt in someway, which could be time-consuming. Moreover, in order to buy some authentic texts, for example, from the newspapers or magazines, they would have to pay for them, so the use of authentic texts was limited.

Third, the institute rules, characteristics of materials, and class size were regarded as external constraints. The institute had a rule for amount of textbook use that teachers who were teaching lower level(level 1 to level 6) were supposed to use the designated textbook for at least 40% of the class time. Thus, teachers used the textbook and authentic materials restrictively. Besides, teachers hesitated to use the authentic texts even if they were aware of the merits of them, and prefer to use them, because authentic texts, representatively newspaper articles, included difficult vocabulary, words used usually in written English, and complicated sentence structure. Sometimes, even though all the necessary things such as authentic texts, procedure of communicative group work were prepared, if the class size was too small because 3-4 people was absent or late,[4] the group work activity was not available.

---

[4] A clas of the institut makes up of 6 to 9 adult learners, and some people are often absent or latedue t their personal matters.

Ⅴ. CONCLUSION

The results of the study showed that teachers' beliefs, which native-speaker(NS) teachers of an English institute in Korea had, a positive influence on their instructional practices even if there were some cases of inconsistency between teachers' expressed beliefs and their actual classroom practices.

All four observed teachers' actual classroom practices were consistent with their expressed beliefs about CLT especially in the areas of the group work activities and grammar instruction. They believed that the group work activities would promote communication in the classroom, and direct grammar teaching would not develop communicative skills, so all four teachers used the group work activities and avoided direct grammar instruction in their classrooms.

An interesting founding of the consistent relationship between teachers' beliefs and actual practices was that two of the four teachers agreed in their attitude scale questionnaires with use of controlled practices or substitution drills, which were not considered communicative activities, and used them in their classrooms. The assumed causes were teachers' learning experience or learners' level.

Teachers tend to teach from their own experience as a student, and they used more structured activities when learners' level was low.

Although most cases were consistent between teachers' expressed beliefs and their actual classroom practices, some discrepancies existed between their beliefs and actual behaviors. Two of the four teachers addressed that authentic texts were useful, but they rarely used them in their classrooms. According to the open-ended questionnaires the four teachers completed, it seemed to be the results of external factors such as the school guidelines about the amount of textbook use, teachers' time to adapt, and the characteristics of the authentic texts that included words for written English or complicated sentence structures.

Even though external factors such as institute teaching guidelines, learners' level, teachers' resources, and their backgrounds might cause some discrepancies between teachers' beliefs and their actual practices, most of the teachers' actual instructional practices were consistent with their expressed beliefs about CLT.

Since teacher's beliefs were fundamental for their actual instructional practices, it should be always considered prior to teaching practice. For this reason, many teacher educators gradually considered investigation of teacher's beliefs as a starting point in teacher training courses. Likewise, researchers and teachers should be aware of the importance of teacher's beliefs.

1. Limitations of this study

First limitation of this study was the small number of participants. A larger sample could have helped this study to get more various ideas about CLT that native-speaker teachers of an institute had, and more causing factors of the discrepancy between teachers' beliefs and practices. Maybe exploration of nine native-speaker teachers through questionnaire and observation showed tendency of beliefs and practices that native-speaker teachers of an institute had regarding CLT, but it could not represent majority of the teachers who are native-speakers of English institutes.

Second limitation was the difficulty of analysis for neutral point of Likert-type of the closed-questionnaire or belief scales(see appendix 1). Middle point could be interpreted variously: 'undecided', 'uncertain', 'unaware', 'unclear', 'middle' between the strongly agreement and disagreement, so the significance of their responses could not be clearly stated.

Third limitation was that all the participants had similar background that they had all TESOL training. Teachers' beliefs of a teacher who had knowledge about TESOL possibly could be influenced by his or her educational background. Teachers' beliefs could largely come from theory rather than their thoughts and experience. Thus results could be different if the study deals with teachers who do not have TESOL background.

A strength of this study, however, was that relationship between teachers' beliefs and practices were explored with participants who were 'native-speakers' and 'teaching at a private institute in Korea' that almost no previous studies dealt with. It is hoped that this study will be a starting point for future research which investigate teachers' beliefs about CLT that native-speaker teachers at an institute in Korea have and the relationship between their beliefs and the practices.

Further research under the same subject, but dividing it into two groups of teachers who teach low level learners and high level ones, would show different results because teachers in this study addressed that lower level students should be taught differently to suit their level and requirements.

It would also be interesting to compare NS teachers with varying educational backgrounds in terms of how they interpret external pressures and reconcile them with their own beliefs.

Bibliography

Allwright, R.(1981). What do we want the teaching materials for *ELT Journal*, 36(1), 5-18.

Allwright, R. L.(1990). *What do we want teaching materials for* In R. Rossner and R. Bolitho, (Eds.), Currents in language teaching. Oxford: Oxford University Press.

Apple, M. and S, Jungck.(1991). "You don't have to be a teacher to teach this unit." Teaching, technology, and gender in the classroom. *American Educational Research Journal.* Summer 1990, 27(2), 227-251

Bachman, L. F.(1990). *Fundamental Considerations in Language Testing. Reading*, MA: Addison-Wesley Publishing Company.

Braithwaite, J.(1999). "Does it matter what I think? An exploration of teachers' constructions of literacy and their classroom practices." Paper presented at the European Conference on Educational Research, Finland(September).

Brophy, J.(1982). How Teacher Influence what is taught and learned in classrooms, *Elementary School Journal*, 83, 1-13.

Borg. M.(2001). Teachers' beliefs. *ELT Journal* 55 / 2. Oxford: Oxford University Press.

Brown, D.(1994). *Teaching by Principles. An interactive approach to language pedagogy.* Prentice Hall Regents.

Brown, D.(2000). *Principles of Language Learning and Teaching.* NY: Addison Wesley Longman, Inc

Calderhead, J.(1996). Teachers: Beliefs and knowledge. In D. C. Berliner & R. C. Calfee (eds.), *Handbook of Educational Psychology* (pp.709-725) New York: Macmillan.

Canale, M., & Swain, M.(1980). "Theoretical bases of communicative approaches to second language teaching and testing." *Applied Linguistics*, 1(1), 1-47.

Carter, K.(1990). "Teachers' knowledge and learning to teach." In W. R. Houston(Ed.) *Handbook of research on teacher education* (pp.291-310). New York: Macmillan.

Chou. J.(2003). Exploring English Teachers' Beliefs and Practical Knowledge about Communicative Language Teaching in EFL Contexts. Retrieved October 10, 2005 from www.hiceducation.org / Edu_Proceedings / Joyce Chiou-hui Chou.pdf

Clark, C. M., and Peterson, P. L.(1986). Teachers' thought processes. In M. C. Wittrock(ed.), *Handbook of Research on Teaching*, 3rd ed. New York: Macmillan. pp 255-96.

Cummins, C. L., Cheek, E. H., and Lindsey, J. D(2004). The relationship between teachers' Literacy Beliefs and their instructional practices: A brief review of the literature for teacher educators. *E-Journal of Teaching & Learning in Divers Settings,* 1(2). Retrieved July 2, 2005, from
http://subr.edu/coeducation/ejournal

Cunningsworth, A.(1998). *Choosing your coursebook.* Oxford: Macmillan Heinemann.

Duffy, G.(1982). "Fighting off the alligators: What research in real classrooms has to say about reading instruction." *Journal of Reading Behavior*, 14, 357-373.

Faerch, Haastrup and Phillipson.(1984). *Learner Language and Language Learning.* Clevedon: Multilingual Matters.

Fenstermacher, G.D.(1978). A philosophical consideration of recent research on teacher effectiveness. In L. S. Schulman(Ed.) *Review of research in education.* Itasca, Il: F. F. Peacock.

Garinger, D.(2001). Textbook Evaluation. *TEFL Web Journal,* Retrieved September 8, 2001, from http://www.teflweb-j.org/v1n1/garinger.html.

Gleespm, A. & Prain, V.(1996). "Should teachers of writing write themselves?: An Australian contribution to the debate." *English Journal*, 85(6), 42-49.

Guariento, W. and Moley, J.(2001). "Text and task authenticity in the EFL classroom." *ELF Jouranl* 55(4), 347-353.

Halliday, M. A. K.(1978). *Language as social semiotic.* Baltimore: University Park Press.

Hedge, T.(2000). *Teaching and Learning in the Language Classroom.* Oxford: Oxford University Press.

Howatt, A. P. R.(1984). *A History of English Language Teaching.* Oxford: Oxford University Press.

Hutchinson, T., and Torres, E.(1994). "The textbook as agent of change." *ELT Journal* 48(4): 315-28.

Hymes, D.(1967). *On Communicative competence.* Unpublished manuscript, University of Pennsylvania.

Hymes, D.(1972). *On Communicative competence.* In C. Brumfit & K. Johnson(Eds.), 1979. The communicative approach to language teaching. Oxford: Oxford University Press.

Johnson, K. E.(1992). "The relationship between teachers' beliefs and practices during literacy instruction for non-native speakers of English." *Journal of Reading Behavior* 24: 83-108.

Johnson, K. E.(1994) "The emerging beliefs and instructional practices of pre-service ESL teachers." *Teaching and Teacher Education*, 10, 439-452.

Karavas-Doukas, E.(1996). "Using attitude scales to investigate teachers' attitudes to the communicative approach." *ELT Journal* 50 / 3. Oxford University Press.

Kenji, Kitao and S. Kathleen Kitao.(1997). Selecting and Developing Teaching / Learning Materials. *The Internet TESL Journal*, Vol.Ⅳ, No.4. Retrieved July 17, 2005, from http://iteslj.org/Articles/Kitao-Materials.html.

Kleinsasser, R. C. and S. J. Savignon.(1991). 'Linguistics, language pedagogy and teachers' technical cultures' in *Georgetown University Round Table in Languages and Linguistics.* Georgetown: Georgetown University Press.

Larsen-Freeman. D.(2000). *Techniques and Principles in Language Teaching.* Oxford: Oxford University Press.

Li, D.(1998). "It's always more difficult than you plan and imagine": Teachers' perceived difficulties in introducing the communicative approach in South Korea. *TESOL Quarterly*, 32(4), 677-702.

Lockhart, C.(1996). Teachers' Beliefs about Writing in Hong Kong Secondary Schools. Perspectives 8, 1(Working Papers of the Department of English, City University of Hong Kong). Retrieved August 20, 2005, from http://sunzi1.lib.hku.hk/hkjo/view/10/10000107.pdf

McGee, L. M., & Tompkins, G. E.(1995). Literature-based reading instruction: What's guiding the instruction? *Language Arts*, 72(6), 405-414.

Morrow, K., and K. Johnson.(1979). *Communicate*. Cambridge: Cambridge University Press.

O'Neill, R.(1982). "Why use textbooks?" *ELT Journal*, 36(2), 104-111.

Pajares, M. F.(19'92). "Teachers' beliefs and educational research: Cleaning up a messy." *Construct Review of Educational Research* 62(3): 307-332.

Peacock, M.(2001). "Pre-service ESL teachers' beliefs about second language learning: a longitudinal study." *System*, 29, 177-195.

Pennington, M., Costa, V., So, S. Shing, J., Hirose, K. and Niedzielski, K.(1996). The teaching of ESL writing in the Asia-Pacific Region: A Cross Country Comparison(submitted for publication).

Richards, J. C.(1993). 'Beyond the textbook: the role of commercial materials in language teaching' *RELC Journal* 24 / 1: 1-15.

Richards, J. C.(2000). *Beyond Training*. Cambridge: Cambridge University.

Richards. J. C.(2001). *Curriculum development in language teaching*. Cambridge: Cambridge University Press.

Richards, J.C.(2004). Communicative Language Teaching Today. Retrived October 10, 2005, from http://www.professorjackrichards.com/pdf/communicative-language-teaching-today-v2.pdf.

Richards, J. C. & Lockhart, C.(1996). *Reflective Teaching in second language classrooms*. Cambridge: Cambridge University.

Richards, J. C., and Mahoney, D.(1996). Teachers and Textbooks: a Survey of Beliefs and Practices. Perspectives 8, 1(Working Papers of the Department of English, City University of Hong Kong). Retrieved August 10, 2005, from http://sunzi1.lib.hku.hk/hkjo/view/10/1000098.pdf

Richards, J. C., and Rodgers, T.(1984). *Approaches and Methods in Language Teaching*. New York: Cambridge University Press.

Richards, J. C., Tung, 'P. & Ng, P.(1992). *The Culture of the English Language Teacher*. City Polytechnic of Hong Kong. Department of English, Research

Report No.6.

Richard, R. D(2004). "A Critical Look at Authentic Materials." *The Journal of Asia TEFL* 1(1): 101-114.

Savignon, S. J.(1983). *Communicative Competence*: *Theory and Classroom Practice.* Reading, MA: Addison-Wesley.

Savignon, S. J.(1991). Communicative Language Teaching: State of the Art. *TESOL Quarterly* 25: 261-277.

Savignon, S. J.(2002). *Communicative Language Teaching*: *Linguistic Theory and Classroom Practice.* Interpreting Communicative Language Teaching: Contexts and Concerns in Teacher Education. London: Yale University Press.

Shavelson, R. J., and Stern, P.(1981). "Research on teachers' pedagogical thoughts, judgments, decisions, and behavior." *Review of Educational Research* 51: 455-98.

Smith, D.(1996). "Teacher decision-making in the adult ESL classroom." In D. Freeman and J. Richards(eds.), *Teacher Learning in Language Teaching.* New York: Cambridge University Press. 197-216.

Studolsky, S.(1989). "Is teaching really by the book?" In P. W. Jackson and S. Haroutunian-Gordon(eds.), *From Socrates to Software*: *The Teacher as Text and the text as Teacher.* Eighty-ninth Yearbook of the National Society for the Study of Education, Part 1. Chicago: University of Chicago Press. 159-84.

Swan, M.(1992). The textbook: Bridge or wall? *Applied Linguistics and Language Teaching* 2(1): 32-5.

Thanasolulas, D.(1999). Coursebook: Take it or leave it. Retrieved August 10, 2005 from http://www.englishclub.com/tefl-articles/coursebook.htm.

Thompson, A.(1992). Teachers' beliefs and conceptions: A synthesis of the research. In D. Grouws(ed.), *Handbook of research on mathematics teaching and learning* (pp.127-146). New York. Macmillan.

Tomlinson, B.(1998). *Materials Development in Language Teaching.* Cambridge: Cambridge Language Teaching Library.

Watcyn-Jones, P.(1981). *Pair Work.* Harmondsworth: Penguin.

Wong, V., Kwok. P., and Choi, N.(1995). "The use of authentic materials at tertiary level." *ELT Journal,* 49(4), 318-322.

Appendix 1.
Questionnaire

* This questionnaire will be used only for the study of TESOL master degree and your name will never be released.

A. Please fill out the following information.

1. Name: _______________________________

   (Email: _______________________________)

2. Nationality:

3. Gender: Female / Male

4. How long have you taught English? ______years

5. Do you have any teacher training? Yes / No

- Degree: Yes / No, If yes, what?

- Diploma: Yes / No, If yes, what?

- Other: Yes / No(Please specify: ______________)

B. Please read the following statements and indicate how much you agree or disagree with the statements by circling the appropriate number with regard to the class(es) you currently teach at the English institute.

	Strongly Disagree 1	2	3	4	Strongly Agree 5
1. Direct grammar explanations in the textbook should be done before communicative activities.	1	2	3	4	5
2. Group work activities promote communication amongst Learners in the classroom.	1	2	3	4	5
3. Since texts from newspapers / magazines / internet are usually beyond learners' level, they are not helpful for learners.	1	2	3	4	5
4. If the teacher focuses on grammatical rules during most of the class time, learners will be able to communicate more effectively.	1	2	3	4	5
5. If students' listening and speaking level is high, grammar instruction is not needed.	1	2	3	4	5
6. Reading passages in textbooks are helpful to learn to Communicate in English.	1	2	3	4	5
7. Group work activities are not effective since it is very difficult for the teacher to prevent learners from using their mother tongue.	1	2	3	4	5
8. Grammar should be taught only as a means to an end not as an end itself.	1	2	3	4	5
9. The teacher should give learners opportunities for free speech practice rather than doing controlled practice	1	2	3	4	5
10. Group work activities promote improvement of language Ability since learners can learn from hearing the language used by other members of the group.	1	2	3	4	5
11. Through repetition of sentences, learners' speaking abilities will improve.	1	2	3	4	5

	Strongly Disagree				Strongly Agree
	1	2	3	4	5
12. Direct instruction in the rules and terminology of grammar is essential if students are to learn to communicate effectively.	1	2	3	4	5
13. Since talking among non-native speakers is not helpful for improvement of language ability, group work activities are not effective.	1	2	3	4	5
14. For learners to improve their ability to use language communicatively, substitution drills(changing a word or a phrase in a sentence) are useful.	1	2	3	4	5
15. Group work activities in the textbook are the most successful when the teacher follows the teacher's manual rather than changing or modifying them.	1	2	3	4	5
16. Since learners have little chance to use English outside the class, group work activities are important in the classroom.	1	2	3	4	5
17. Once students master the rules of grammar, they become better communicator.	1	2	3	4	5
18. Group work activities in the textbook can be changed (added to or omitted) by the teacher.	1	2	3	4	5
19. Even if learners' comprehension level is low with authentic 'real-life' texts, using them will help learners' communicative abilities.	1	2	3	4	5
20. Grammar explanations are necessary for both high and low level students.	1	2	3	4	5
21. Group work activities are not effective to improve language skills since it is very difficult for the teacher to monitor students.	1	2	3	4	5
22. In a language classroom which focuses on communication, knowledge of grammar rules does not guarantee ability being able to use the language.	1	2	3	4	5
23. For learners to be effective communicators outside the class, they should learn language through authentic texts.	1	2	3	4	5

	Strongly Disagree 1	2	3	4	Strongly Agree 5
24. Learners develop their language abilities by expressing their thoughts and opinion in their own words.	1	2	3	4	5
25. Without grammar explanations, speaking or listening activities in the textbook can be effective for improving communicative ability.	1	2	3	4	5
26. The use of authentic materials will develop learners' language ability.	1	2	3	4	5
27. Question-answer practice in a pair using a list of fixed questions is an effective activity to improve communicative ability.	1	2	3	4	5
28. Since texts from newspapers / magazines / internet are not written For language teaching, they are not appropriate for teaching materials.	1	2	3	4	5
29. Teaching grammar during communicative activity is more effective than doing grammar activities separately.	1	2	3	4	5
30. Repeating dialogues in pairs does not improve communicative ability.	1	2	3	4	5

Appendix 2.

Open-ended questionnaire

Name:

- Do you teach grammar(almost) every class? Yes / No
- How and when do you think grammar teaching should be done in a class which focuses on communicative language skills?

- Do you think repetition of dialogues, substitution drills, and controlled activities improve communicative ability? Yes / No
- What kind of activity do you think promotes communicative language skills?

- Do you think group work activities are effective in promoting class communication? Yes / No
- Why do you use group work activities?

If you do not use group work activities, why?

- Do you usually use the textbook? Yes / No, Do you think the textbook is effective for promoting for communicative language skills?
- Do you use outside materials like newspapers or magazines? If so, what kind and why?
- What are the advantages and disadvantages of using these kinds of materials to teach communicative skills?

Appendix 3.

Classroom observation sheet

- Instructor:
- Learners level:
- Date of observation:
- Time:

1. Grammar instruction: ____min

No change from the textbook :	Change from the textbook :	Use of other course book :	No textbook :	Others :
min	min	min	min	min

1.1 Was direct grammar explanation in the textbook done before communicative activities? Yes / No

1.2 Did the teacher focus on grammatical rules of the language during the most of class time? Yes / No

1.3 Did the teacher teach grammar during communicative rather than doing grammar activities separately? Yes / No

1.4 Did the teacher give direct instruction in the rules and terminology of grammar? Yes / No

2. Group work activities: min

No change from the textbook	Change from the textbook	Use of other course book	No textbook	Others
:	:	:	:	:
min	min	min	min	min

2.1 Did the teacher follow the group activities in the textbook as instructed in the teacher's manual? Yes / No

2.2 Did the teacher change(add to or omit) the group work activities in the textbook? Yes / No

2.3 Did the teacher monitor or participate in the learners' group activity? Yes / No

3. Authentic text usage: min

3.1 Where the authentic texts from? Newspapers(   ), Magazines(   ), Internet(   ), Others:

3.2 What activities did the class do with the authentic texts?

Exchange of opinions about the texts(   )

Discussion on content before / during / after reading(   )

Vocabulary study(   )

Further discussion on the related topic(   )

Other:

4. Types of activities

Activity	No change from the textbook	Change from the textbook	Use of other course book	Other printed materials	Others
4.1 Repetition of sentences	min	min	min	min	min
4.2 Controlled practice	min	min	min	min	min
4.3 Substitution drills	min	min	min	min	min
4.4 Questions-answer practice in pairs	min	min	min	min	min
4.5 Repeating dialogues in pairs	min	min	min	min	min
4.6 Free speech practice	min	min	min	min	min
4.7 Others:	min	min	min	min	min

Abstract

An exploratory study about the relationship between teacher's beliefs about Communicative Language Teaching(CLT) and their instructional practices

HyonSuk Cho
TESOL Graduate School
Dankook University

Advisor: Michele Milner

Despite the popularity of Communicative Language Teaching (CLT) at language institutes in Korea, not all classes are always conducted in a communicative way. This study explores the relationship between teachers' expressed beliefs about CLT and their actual classroom practices. Research about teachers' beliefs shows that teachers' beliefs and their instructional practices are often consistent, however, inconsistencies have also been observed due to the presence of external factors such as teaching guidelines or learners' background. In order to understand teachers' beliefs about CLT and their practices within the EFL context of an

English language institute in Korea, a Likert-type attitude scale was developed. To compare teachers' actual practices with their expressed beliefs, classroom observations were carried out, and a follow-up, open-ended questionnaire was used to explore discrepancies between expressed beliefs and observed practices. The study found that there was a positive relationship between teachers' expressed beliefs and the observed practices, however, external factors such as teaching guidelines of the institute, teachers' backgrounds, learners' levels, and teachers' resources also had some influence on the teachers' practices.

• 저자 •   조현숙

- 단국대학교 TESOL 대학원 석사
- University of Pennsylvania, Graduate School of Education, TESOL 석사
- 박정 어학원 EDi 영어 교재 집필
- 기업체 영어 회화 출강
- YBMsisa.com 영어 강의 기획

의사소통을 위한 언어 교육에 대한 원어민 교사의 생각과 실제 행동 관계 연구

• 초판 인쇄	2007년 4월 20일
• 초판 발행	2007년 4월 20일
• 지 은 이	조현숙
• 펴 낸 이	채종준
• 펴 낸 곳	한국학술정보㈜
	경기도 파주시 교하읍 문발리 526-2
	파주출판문화정보산업단지
	전화 031) 908-3181(대표) · 팩스 031) 908-3189
	홈페이지 http://www.kstudy.com
	e-mail(출판사업팀사업부) publish@kstudy.com
• 등 록	제일산-115호(2000. 6. 19)
• 가 격	5,000원

ISBN   978-89-534-6593-0 93740 (Paper Book)
       978-89-534-6594-7 98740 (e-Book)